KNITTING
Aran Sweaters

© 1992 Lyric Books Ltd
PO Box 152, Mill Hill, London NW7, England

First published in 1992

ISBN 0 7111 0014 4

Printed in Belgium by
Proost International Book Production

Introduction

HARMONY CLASS is for everyone. Beginners will find the classes friendly and instructional, experienced knitters will find them challenging and informative.

Step-by-step instructions for some of the most common Aran techniques are followed by knitting instructions for a classic Sweater knitted in double moss stitch. This is a stitch which is used so often in Aran knitting it embodies the spirit of Ireland and its knitting in every stitch!

The classic Sweater is the basis for all the variations that can be made by combining double moss stitch with traditional panels. The third section tells you how you can put these combinations together. We have included some suggested combinations of panels to inspire you but do plan your own designs - your only limitation being whether it is possible to fit your planned design into the desired width of the material! Remember - **the choice is yours.**

Basic knitting techniques which will be of particular interest to the less experienced knitter follow, and we finish with some hints and tips which could be helpful to all of you.

Incidentally, we would be glad to hear from **you** if you have tips which we can add to future editions of our books and which would interest other knitters.

Contents

Aran Knitting

Origins

The Isles of Aran are set in the Atlantic Ocean at the mouth of Galway Bay off the west coast of Ireland. The environment is harsh. The soil is poor. The people eked a living from subsistence farming and the sea.

Warm, protective and practical clothing was essential in this windswept climate where only sheep could provide the raw material. Hence the traditional Aran sweater developed. The women spun the yarn. The men knitted, developing patterns and stitches from their skills as fishermen and sailors. The twisting and braiding techniques learned from making ropes and rigging formed the basis of the cables, ropes and plaits in their knitting patterns.

Aran stitches are traditional, often religious in origin. The Trinity Stitch, created by working three stitches from one and one stitch from three, is thought to signify the Holy Trinity, (Father, Son and Holy Ghost).

Patterns were not recorded. They were learnt only by example passing from generation to generation.

Yarn

Traditionally, Aran garments were knitted from unscoured wool to retain the natural greases, thus ensuring that they were waterproof. The tradition remains and Aran garments are normally knitted in thickish, creamy white wool whose properties still make them ideal for outdoor wear. It is an excellent insulator and absorbs moisture while keeping the wearer warm and dry. Wool is also malleable so that it can be steamed into shape. This is important for some more intricate patterns as they require light steam to lie flat. Synthetic yarns that do not possess this quality are sometimes unsuitable for Aran designs. Nevertheless, sweaters can take on an original look if knitted in non-traditional yarns such as mohair or cotton or varying colours. **The choice is yours.**

Cables and Stitches

The basis of many Aran patterns is the simple cable. A cable needle is used to move one stitch or a group of stitches over or behind another. When knitted on a plain background this resembles rope.

Cables

Cables are achieved by moving one group of knit stitches over another. Here the cable panel consists of four stitches in stocking stitch against a reverse stocking stitch background.

C4B (Cable 4 Back)

1 On a right side row, work to the position of the cable panel and slip the next two stitches on to the cable needle.

2 With the stitches on the cable needle held at the back of the work, knit the next two stitches from the left-hand needle.

3 Now knit the two stitches from the cable needle to produce the crossover.

Leaving the first set of stitches at the back of the work produces a cable that crosses to the right.

C4F (Cable 4 Front) ◣◥◣◥

1 On a right side row, work to the position of the cable panel and slip the next two stitches on to the cable needle, leaving it at the front of the work.

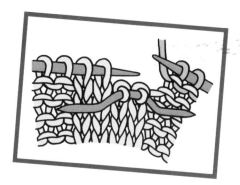

2 Working behind the cable needle, knit the next two stitches from the left-hand needle.

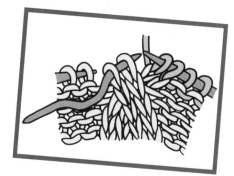

3 Now knit the two stitches from the cable needle to produce the crossover.

Leaving the first set of stitches at the front of the work produces a cable that crosses to the left.

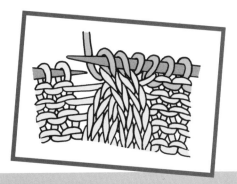

The number of stitches crossed can be varied to make larger and smaller cables. The number of rows between each crossover can also vary.

Once the basic cable technique has been mastered it can be used to produce many variations of the simple rope pattern.

Twisting Stitches

Lattice effects and more complicated cable patterns can be worked by using twist stitches. These are similar to cables but the effect is achieved using knit and purl stitches, not just knit stitches.

Here two knit stitches are moved in a diagonal direction across a background of reverse st st.

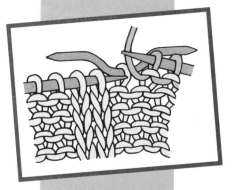

T3B (Twist 3 Back)

1 On a right side row, work to one stitch before the two knit stitches. Slip the next stitch on to a cable needle and leave it at the back of the work.

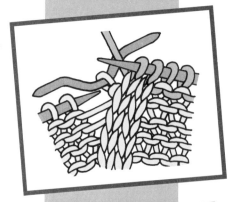

2 Knit the next two stitches from the left-hand needle.

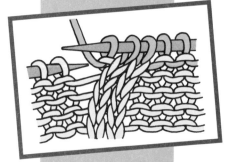

3 Now purl the stitch from the cable needle to produce a twist to the right.

T3F (Twist 3 Front)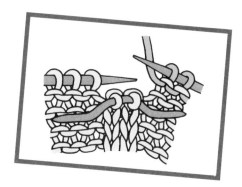

1 On a right side row, work to the two knit stitches. Slip these two stitches on to a cable needle and leave them at the front of the work.

2 Purl the next stitch from the left-hand needle.

3 Knit the two stitches from the cable needle to produce a twist to the left.

The examples given show two stitches twisted to the right (T3B) and left (T3F) over a background of reverse stocking stitch.

Like cables the number of stitches within a twist can vary. Also twist stitches can be worked over a variety of background stitches, usually stocking stitch or reverse stocking stitch.

Stitches can be cabled and twisted in countless knit and purl combinations. However, the basic principle is always the same.

Re-Crossing Cables

A common mistake which occurs in the working of Cable or Aran patterns is that you find you have crossed a cable in the wrong direction several rows below. This is easily put right and gives you the opportunity of practising a technique that can be useful in many other ways. If you have crossed a cable of 6 stitches (three over three) in the wrong direction, work as follows:

1 Carefully cut the centre stitch of the top three stitches of the row at the point where the cable crosses over. Undo these three top stitches leaving the ends of yarn loose on either side.

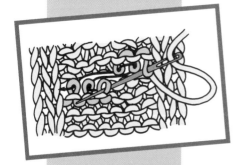

2 Lift up the underneath three stitches which in fact now become the top ones and graft the original three stitches back in position underneath (see page 47), from wrong side following diagram, thus correcting the slope of the cable.

Pattern and Designs

Double Moss Stitch Sweater

To Fit

Bust/Chest sizes	85/90	95/100	105/110	cm
	34/36	38/40	42/44	ins
Finished measurement	104	115	127	cm
	41¹/₂	46	51	ins
Length to Shoulder	64	68	72	cm
	25¹/₄	26³/₄	28¹/₄	ins
Sleeve length	45	47	48	cm
	17³/₄	18¹/₂	19	ins

Materials

Aran thickness yarn (wool)	800	1000	1150	grams
Aran thickness yarn (acrylic)	600	700	900	approx.

Pair needles each size 5mm (No.6) and 4mm (No.8)

Tension

19 sts and 26 rows = 10 cm [4 ins] square measured over double moss stitch using larger needles. See Tension on page 44.

For notes, abbreviations and details of how to follow stitch charts see pages 42 and 43.

The quantities of yarn stated are based on average requirements and are therefore approximate. For yarn equivalents see page 48.

Special Abbreviations

Inc 2 = work (p1, k1, p1) all into next st.

Back

Using smaller needles cast on 85(95-105) sts.

1st row (right side): K1, *p1, k1; rep from * to end.
2nd row: P1, *k1, p1; rep from * to end.
Rep the last 2 rows until rib measures 8 cm [3 ins] ending with a right side row.

Next row (increase): Rib 6(4-10), *Inc 2, rib 11(13-11); rep from * to last 7(7-11) sts, Inc 2, rib to end. 99(109-121) sts.

Change to larger needles and commence pattern.

1st row: P1, *k1, p1; rep from * to end.
2nd row: K1, *p1, k1; rep from * to end.
3rd row: K1, *p1, k1; rep from * to end.
4th row: P1, *k1, p1; rep from * to end.

These 4 rows form double moss stitch pattern ★. Keeping pattern correct continue until Back measures 64(68-72) cm [25¹/₄(26³/₄-28¹/₄) ins] or required length to shoulder ending with a wrong side row.

Shape Shoulders

Next row: Cast off 35(39-44) sts, work until there are 29(31-33) sts on right-hand needle, cast off remaining 35(39-44) sts. Slip remaining 29(31-33) sts on to a holder for neckband.

Front

Work as given for Back to ★. Keeping pattern correct, continue until Front is 23(27-31) rows shorter than Back to shoulder, thus ending with a right side row.

Shape Neck

Next row: Work 43(48-54) sts, turn and complete this side first. Keeping pattern correct dec 1 st at neck edge on next 5 rows, then following 3(4-5) alt rows. 35(39-44) sts remain. Work 11(13-15) rows straight thus ending with a wrong side row. Cast off.

Slip next 13 sts at centre on to a holder for neckband. With wrong side facing rejoin yarn to neck edge of remaining 43(48-54) sts and work to end. Dec 1 st at neck edge on next 5 rows, then following 3(4-5) alt rows. 35(39-44) sts remain. Work 11(13-15) rows straight thus ending with a wrong side row. Cast off.

Sleeves

Using smaller needles cast on 41(47-51) sts and work 8 cm [3 ins] in k1, p1 rib as given for Back ending with a right side row.

Next row (increase): Rib 4(2-4), *Inc 2, rib 7(9-9); rep from * to last 5(5-7) sts, Inc 2, rib to end. 51(57-61) sts.

Change to larger needles and work 4 rows in double moss stitch as given for Back.

Bringing extra sts into double moss stitch, inc 1 st at each end of next and every following 4th row until there are 63(77-107) sts.

1st (2nd) sizes only: Inc 1 st at each end of every following 5th row until there are 87(97) sts.

All sizes: Work straight until sleeve measures 45(47-48) cm [17³/4(18¹/2-19) ins] or required length ending with a wrong side row. Cast off.

Finishing and Neckband

Press pieces according to instructions on ball band. Join left shoulder seam.

Neckband: Using smaller needles and with right side facing, knit across sts on holder at back neck decreasing 1 st at centre, pick up and k20(23-26) sts down left front slope, knit across sts on holder at front neck and pick up and k20(23-26) sts up right front slope. 81(89-97) sts.

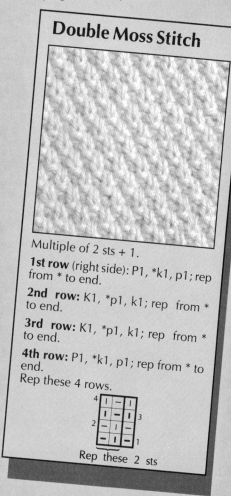

Double Moss Stitch

Multiple of 2 sts + 1.

1st row (right side): P1, *k1, p1; rep from * to end.

2nd row: K1, *p1, k1; rep from * to end.

3rd row: K1, *p1, k1; rep from * to end.

4th row: P1, *k1, p1; rep from * to end.

Rep these 4 rows.

Rep these 2 sts

Starting with a 2nd row, work 8 cm [3 ins] in k1, p1 rib as given for Back. Slip sts on to a length of yarn.

Join right shoulder seam and ends of neckband. Fold neckband in half to inside and slip stitch loosely in place, allowing for stretch and taking care to catch every stitch.

Fold sleeves in half lengthways and mark centre of cast off edge. Sew sleeve to side edge placing centre at shoulder seam.

Note: Armhole should measure approximately 23(25-28) cm [9(10-11 1/4) ins]. Join side and sleeve seams. Press seams if required.

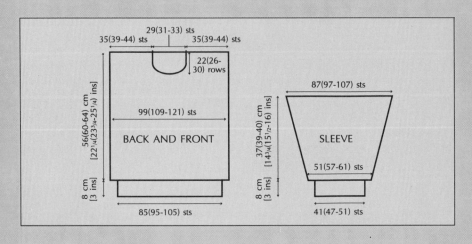

Abbreviations

For standard abbreviations, notes and details of how follow stitch charts see pages 42 and 43.

T3B (Twist 3 Back) = slip next st on to cable needle and hold at back of work, knit next 2 sts from left-hand needle, then purl st from cable needle.

T3F (Twist 3 Front) = slip next 2 sts on to cable needle and hold at front of work, purl next st from left-hand needle, then knit sts from cable needle.

C4B (Cable 4 Back) = slip next 2 sts on to cable needle and hold at back of work, knit next 2 sts from left-hand needle, then knit sts from cable needle.

C4F (Cable 4 Front) = slip next 2 sts on to cable needle and hold at front of work, knit next 2 sts from left-hand needdle, then knit sts from cable needle.

C4R (Cable 4 Right) = slip next st on to cable needle and hold at back of work, knit next 3 sts from left-hand needle, then knit st from cable needle.

C4L (Cross 4 Left) = slip next 3 sts on to cable needle and hold at front of work, knit next st from left-hand needle, then knit sts from cable needle.

T4B (Twist 4 Back) = slip next 2 sts on to cable needle and hold at back of work, knit next 2 sts from left-hand needle, then purl sts from cable needle.

T4F (Twist 4 Front) = slip next 2 sts on to cable needle and hold at front of work, purl next 2 sts from left-hand needle, then knit sts from cable needle.

T4R (Twist 4 Right) = slip next st on to cable needle and hold at back of work, knit next 3 sts from left-hand needle, then purl st from cable needle.

T4L (Twist 4 Left) = slip next 3 sts on to cable needle and hold at front of work, purl next st from left-hand needle, then knit sts from cable needle.

C6B (Cable 6 Back) = slip next 3 sts on to cable needle and hold at back of work, knit next 3 sts from left-hand needle, then knit sts from cable needle.

C6F (Cable 6 Front) = slip next 3 sts on to cable needle and hold at front of work, knit next 3 sts from left-hand needle, then knit sts from cable needle.

C7B (Cable 7 Back) = slip next 4 sts on to cable needle and hold at back of work, knit next 3 sts from left-hand needle, then knit sts from cable needle.

C8B (Cable 8 Back) = slip next 4 sts on to cable needle and hold at back of work, knit next 4 sts from left-hand needle, then knit sts from cable needle.

C8F (Cable 8 Front) = slip next 4 sts on to cable needle and hold at front of work, knit next 4 sts from left-hand needle, then knit sts from cable needle.

HARMONY CLASS gives you all the information you need to adapt the classic double moss stitch pattern into one of the designs shown on the following pages - or into any other combination of panels which will fit.

Aran panels are made by crossing one or more stitches over other stitches and this has the effect of tightening the fabric. For this reason it is usually necessary to add (increase) a few extra stitches at the point where the panel is to be placed. For example - we knitted Panel H (shown on page 27) and it measured 8.5 cm [3¼ ins] in width, and used 26 stitches. The same width in the same yarn in double moss stitch only used 17 stitches, and therefore you must increase 9 stitches at the required position before you start that panel, otherwise the fabric you knit will be narrower than you require.

To fit panels into the classic pattern you must first knit a sample of double moss stitch to give you your 'basic' tension (see page 11). All the swatches and garments in this book were worked in the same yarn, and based on our basic tension over double moss stitch of 19 stitches to 10 cm [4 ins] in width. If you can match this tension you will be able to work from the measurements we have given. If in doubt read the paragraph relating to Tension on page 44 and adjust your needle size accordingly.

The Lady's Sweater illustrated opposite has two OXO cables (Panel G given on page 24), on one side of the front while the back and sleeves are knitted in double moss stitch as the classic pattern. The number of stitches cast on for the ribbing was the same as for the classic sweater, but on the last row of the rib, stitches were increased at the position where the panels were to be placed. These additional stitches have to be eliminated in the neck or shoulder shaping, depending on where the panel is placed. This is easy provided you always think of each of those panels as a block of a known number of stitches. It may help to work panels between slip markers (see page 41). **Do** make notes to remind you what you have done as you go along. It doesn't matter how scruffy they are - they are for your eyes only, but they will help.

Don't worry too much about the exact finished measurement. Aran knitting is very flexible, and in these days of comfortable, easy-wear clothes it is less important if you have a couple more or less stitches to make your design work. Length measurements, which can be important, are easily adjusted.

Stitch Tables

With each of our 'inspirational' sketches we give you a table showing how the number of stitches for that particular

combination of panels and double moss stitch (dms) was worked out.

The top line of the table indicates the stitches used.

The darker tinted ▨ line gives the number of stitches required for each panel.

The light tinted ☐ line gives the number of stitches that would be required for each panel if worked in dms.

From the table you can see that to work Panel G 10 stitches are needed instead of the 7 stitches in dms. Therefore three stitches have to be increased before starting each Panel G.

Note: Use slip markers (see page 41) to indicate the position of the cable panels.

For notes and abbreviations see pages 13, 42 and 43.

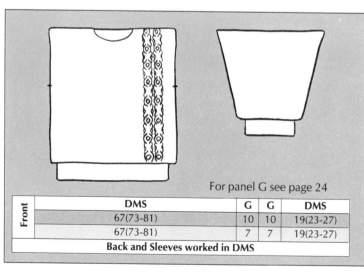

For panel G see page 24

Front	DMS	G	G	DMS
	67(73-81)	10	10	19(23-27)
	67(73-81)	7	7	19(23-27)
	Back and Sleeves worked in DMS			

design 2

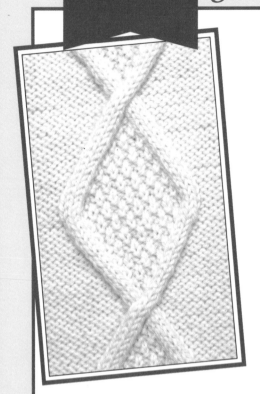

Panel A

23 sts measures 9 cm [3 1/2 ins].

1st row (right side): P7, C4R, p1, C4L, p7.

2nd row: K7, p4, k1, p4, k7.

3rd row: P6, C4R, p1, k1, p1, C4L, p6.

4th row: K6, p4, k1, p1, k1, p4, k6.

5th row: P5, C4R, p1, [k1, p1] twice, C4L, p5.

6th row: K5, p4, k1, [p1, k1] twice, p4, k5.

7th row: P4, C4R, p1, [k1, p1] 3 times, C4L, p4.

8th row: K4, p4, k1, [p1, k1] 3 times, p4, k4.

9th row: P3, C4R, p1, [k1, p1] 4 times, C4L, p3.

10th row: K3, p4, k1, [p1, k1] 4 times, p4, k3.

11th row: P2, C4R, p1, [k1, p1] 5 times, C4L, p2.

12th row: K2, p4, k1, [p1, k1] 5 times, p4, k2.

13th row: P1,C4R, p1, [k1, p1] 6 times, C4L, p1.

14th row: K1, p4, k1, [p1, k1] 6 times, p4, k1.

15th row: P1, k3, p1, [k1, p1] 7 times, k3, p1.

16th row: K1, p3, k1, [p1, k1] 7 times, p3, k1.

17th row: P1, T4L, p1, [k1, p1] 6 times, T4R, p1.

18th row: K2, p3, k1, [p1, k1] 6 times, p3, k2.

19th row: P2, T4L, p1, [k1, p1] 5 times, T4R, p2.

20th row: K3, p3, k1, [p1, k1] 5 times, p3, k3.

21st row: P3, T4L, p1, [k1, p1] 4 times, T4R, p3.

22nd row: K4, p3, k1, [p1, k1] 4 times, p3, k4.

23rd row: P4, T4L, p1, [k1, p1] 3 times, T4R, p4.

24th row: K5, p3, k1, [p1, k1] 3 times, p3, k5.

25th row: P5, T4L, p1, [k1, p1] twice, T4R, p5.

26th row: K6, p3, k1, [p1, k1] twice, p3, k6.

27th row: P6, T4L, p1, k1, p1, T4R, p6.

28th row: K7, p3, k1, p1, k1, p3, k7.

29th row: P7, T4L, p1, T4R, p7.

30th row: K8, p3, k1, p3, k8.

31st row: P8, C7B, p8.

32nd row: K8, p7, k8.

Rep these 32 rows.

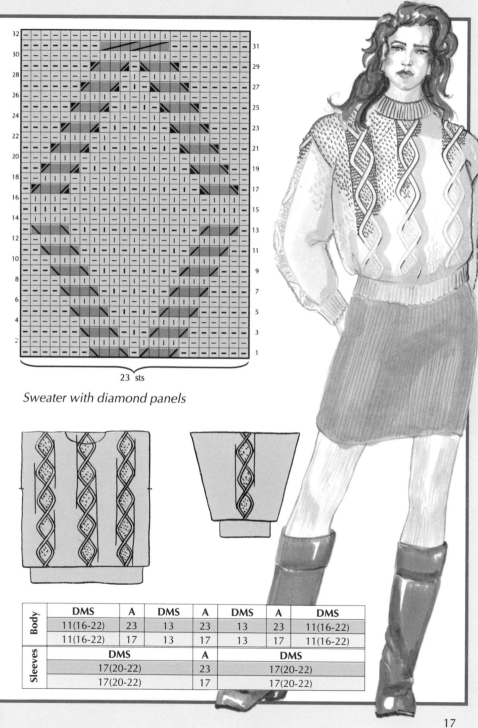

Sweater with diamond panels

23 sts

		DMS	A	DMS	A	DMS	A	DMS
Body		11(16-22)	23	13	23	13	23	11(16-22)
		11(16-22)	17	13	17	13	17	11(16-22)
Sleeves		DMS			A		DMS	
		17(20-22)			23		17(20-22)	
		17(20-22)			17		17(20-22)	

Panel B (on right of photograph)

8 sts measures 2.5 cm [1 inch].

1st row (right side): P1, k6, p1.

2nd row: K1, p6, k1.

3rd row: P1, C6B, p1.

4th row: K1, p6, k1.

Rep these 4 rows.

Panel C (on left of photograph)

Work as given for Panel B **but** working C6F in place of C6B.

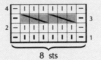

With these three sweaters we show some of the possibilities open to you using just one simple rope cable spaced or grouped in different positions.

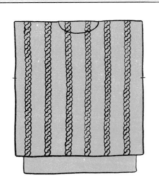

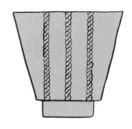

	DMS	B	DMS	B	DMS	B	DMS	B	DMS	B	DMS	B	DMS
Body	7(12-18)	8	11	8	11	8	11	8	11	8	11	8	7(12-18)
	7(12-18)	5	11	5	11	5	11	5	11	5	11	5	7(12-18)

	DMS	B	DMS	B	DMS	B	DMS
Sleeves	7(10-12)	8	11	8	11	8	7(10-12)
	7(10-12)	5	11	5	11	5	7(10-12)

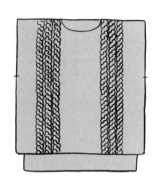

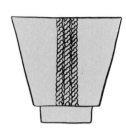

Body	DMS	C	C	C	DMS	B	B	B	DMS
	20(23-27)	8	8	8	29(33-37)	8	8	8	20(23-27)
	20(23-27)	5	5	5	29(33-37)	5	5	5	20(23-27)

Sleeves	DMS		B	B	B	DMS	
	18(21-23)		8	8	8	18(21-23)	
	18(21-23)		5	5	5	18(21-23)	

Body	DMS	B	B	B	B	B	DMS
	37(42-48)	8	8	8	8	8	37(42-48)
	37(42-48)	5	5	5	5	5	37(42-48)
Sleeves worked in DMS							

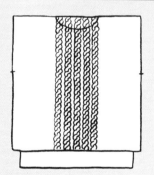

design 6

Panel D

Multiple of 8 sts + 10. 26 sts measures 9 cm [2 1/2 ins].

1st row (right side): P3, C4B, *p4, C4B; rep from * to last 3 sts, p3.

2nd row: K3, p4, *k4, p4; rep from * to last 3 sts, k3.

3rd row: P1, *T4B, T4F; rep from * to last st, p1.

4th row: K1, p2, k4, *p4, k4; rep from * to last 3 sts, p2, k1.

5th row: P1, k2, p4, *C4B, p4; rep from * to last 3 sts, k2, p1.

6th row: As 4th row.

7th row: P1, *T4F, T4B; rep from * to last st, p1.

8th row: As 2nd row.

Rep these 8 rows.

The trellis pattern when worked over more repeats gives a very different look see page 28.
For this sweater we have used a two repeat trellis with the rope cables each side.

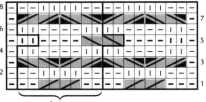

Rep these 8 sts

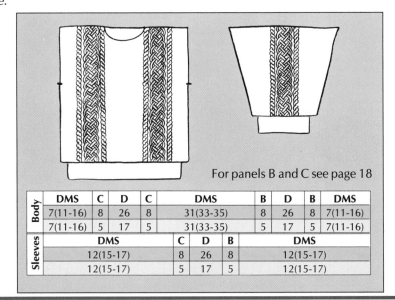

For panels B and C see page 18

Body	DMS	C	D	C	DMS	B	D	B	DMS
	7(11-16)	8	26	8	31(33-35)	8	26	8	7(11-16)
	7(11-16)	5	17	5	31(33-35)	5	17	5	7(11-16)

Sleeves	DMS	C	D	B	DMS
	12(15-17)	8	26	8	12(15-17)
	12(15-17)	5	17	5	12(15-17)

Sweater with plait cables

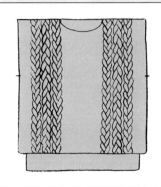 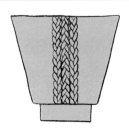

Body	DMS	F	E	F	DMS	F	E	F	DMS
	10(14-19)	14	14	14	31(33-35)	14	14	14	10(14-19)
	10(14-19)	8	8	8	31(33-35)	8	8	8	10(14-19)

Sleeves	DMS	F	E	F	DMS
	14(17-19)	14	14	14	14(17-19)
	14(17-19)	8	8	8	14(17-19)

Panel E (on right of photograph)

14 sts measures 4 cm [1 1/2 ins].

1st row (right side): P1, k12, p1.
2nd row: K1, p12, k1.
3rd row: P1, k4, C8B, p1.
4th row: K1, p12, k1.
5th and 6th rows: As 1st and 2nd rows.
7th row: P1, C8F, k4, p1.
8th row: K1, p12, k1.
Rep these 8 rows.

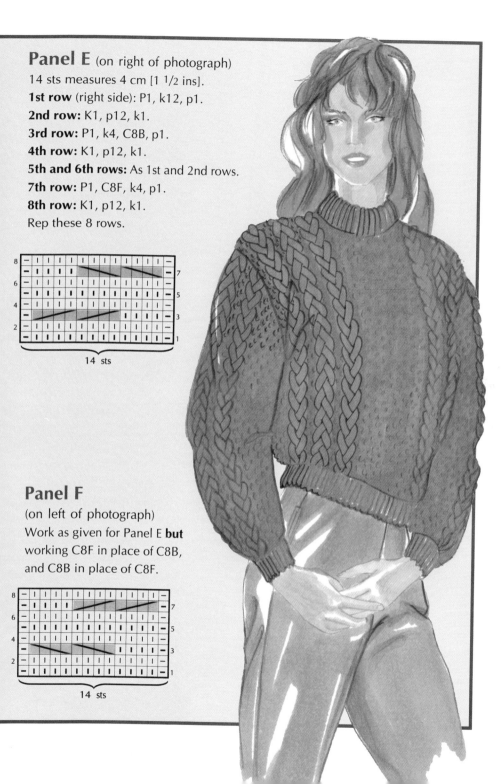

14 sts

Panel F

(on left of photograph)
Work as given for Panel E **but**
working C8F in place of C8B,
and C8B in place of C8F.

14 sts

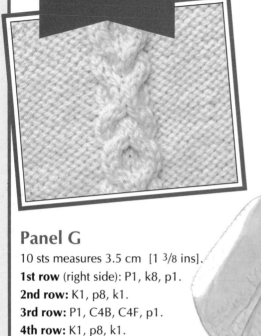

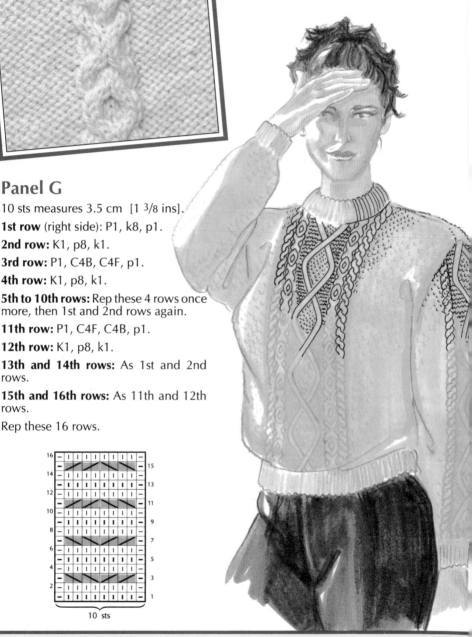

Panel G

10 sts measures 3.5 cm [1 3/8 ins].

1st row (right side): P1, k8, p1.

2nd row: K1, p8, k1.

3rd row: P1, C4B, C4F, p1.

4th row: K1, p8, k1.

5th to 10th rows: Rep these 4 rows once more, then 1st and 2nd rows again.

11th row: P1, C4F, C4B, p1.

12th row: K1, p8, k1.

13th and 14th rows: As 1st and 2nd rows.

15th and 16th rows: As 11th and 12th rows.

Rep these 16 rows.

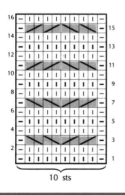

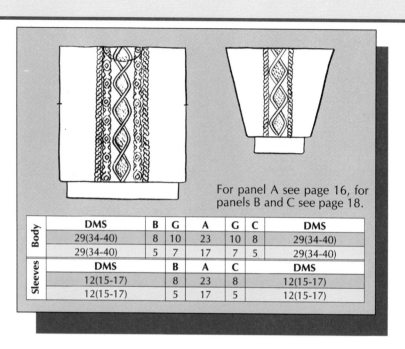

For panel A see page 16, for panels B and C see page 18.

	DMS	B	G	A	G	C	DMS
Body	29(34-40)	8	10	23	10	8	29(34-40)
	29(34-40)	5	7	17	7	5	29(34-40)
Sleeves	DMS	B	A	C			DMS
	12(15-17)	8	23	8			12(15-17)
	12(15-17)	5	17	5			12(15-17)

This sweater combines the OXO cable with the diamond panel and robe cables which appear on earlier pages.

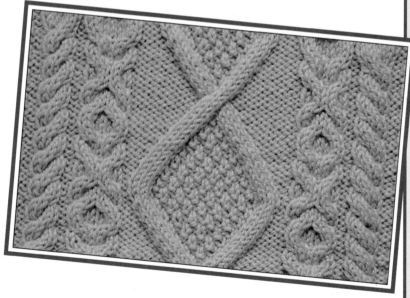

This sweater combines the plait cable with a lattic panel to give an interesting centre panel.

For panel F see page 23

Body	DMS	F	F	DMS	H	DMS	F	F	DMS
	16(21-27)	14	14	9	26	9	14	14	16(21-27)
	16(21-27)	8	8	9	17	9	8	8	16(21-27)
					Sleeves worked in DMS				

Panel H

26 sts measures 8.5 cm [3 1/4 ins].

1st row (right side): P3, C4B, [p4, C4B] twice, p3.

2nd row: K3, p4, [k4, p4] twice, k3.

3rd row: P2, T3B, [T4F, T4B] twice, T3F, p2.

4th row: K2, p2, k3, p4, k4, p4, k3, p2, k2.

5th row: P1, T3B, p3, C4F, p4, C4F, p3, T3F, p1.

6th row: K1, p2, k4, [p4, k4] twice, p2, k1.

7th row: P1, k2, p3, T3B, T4F, T4B, T3F, p3, k2, p1.

8th row: K1, [p2, k3] twice, p4, [k3, p2] twice, k1.

9th row: P1, [k2, p3] twice, C4B, [p3, k2] twice, p1.

10th row: As 8th row.

11th row: P1, k2, p3, T3F, T4B, T4F, T3B, p3, k2, p1.

12th row: As 6th row.

13th row: P1, T3F, p3, C4F, p4, C4F, p3, T3B, p1.

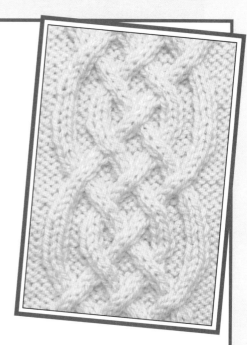

14th row: As 4th row.

15th row: P2, T3F, [T4B, T4F] twice, T3B, p2.

16th row: As 2nd row.

Rep these 16 rows.

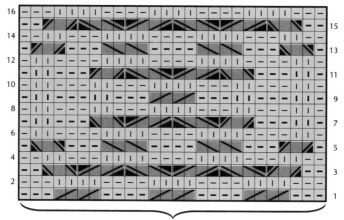

26 sts

For panel A see page 16, for panels B and C see page 18, for panel D see page 21.

	DMS	C	A	C	D	B	A	B	DMS
Body	12(14-20)	8	23	8	34(42-42)	8	23	8	12(14-20)
	12(14-20)	5	17	5	21(27-27)	5	17	5	12(14-20)

	DMS	C	A	B	DMS
Sleeves	12(15-17)	8	23	8	12(15-17)
	12(15-17)	5	17	5	12(15-17)

For more confident knitters this is a lovely combination of cable panels - but also shown is a sweater with just the centre section cabled.

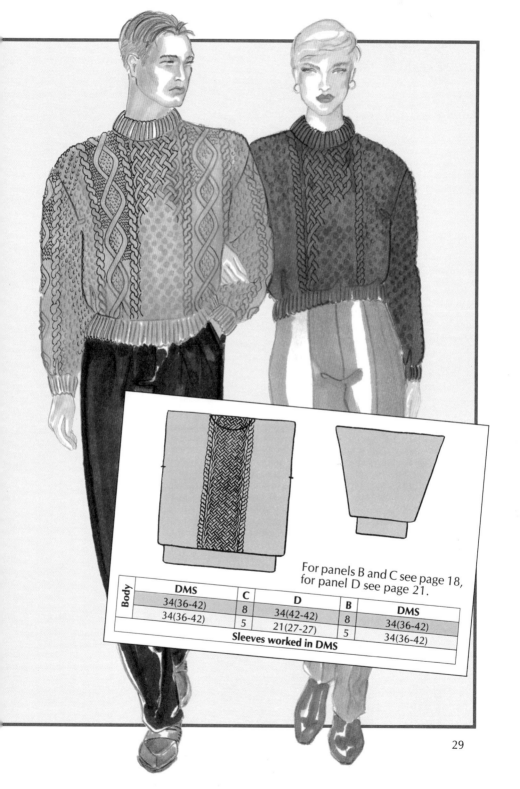

For panels B and C see page 18, for panel D see page 21.

Body	DMS	C	D	B	DMS
	34(36-42)	8	34(42-42)	8	34(36-42)
	34(36-42)	5	21(27-27)	5	34(36-42)
			Sleeves worked in DMS		

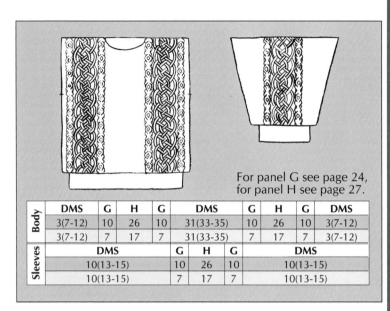

For panel G see page 24,
for panel H see page 27.

Body	DMS	G	H	G	DMS	G	H	G	DMS
	3(7-12)	10	26	10	31(33-35)	10	26	10	3(7-12)
	3(7-12)	7	17	7	31(33-35)	7	17	7	3(7-12)

Sleeves	DMS		G	H	G		DMS	
	10(13-15)		10	26	10		10(13-15)	
	10(13-15)		7	17	7		10(13-15)	

This sweater shows panels of the lattice and OXO cables.

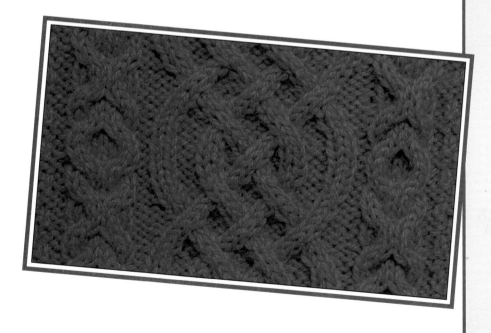

Knitting Know How

In the following pages we give detailed instructions and diagrams for working basic stitches, understanding diagrams and working from pattern instructions.

Equipment

Knitting needles are used in pairs to produce a flat knitted fabric. They range in size from 2mm to 17mm in diameter. It is useful to have a range of sizes so that tension swatches can be knitted on various needles and compared. They are also available in various lengths - choose a length that will comfortably hold the stitches required for each project. To produce a tubular fabric or flat rounds (such as circular shawls) use **double-pointed needles** (sold in sets of four or five), or **circular needles** (two needle points joined by a flexible length of plastic).

Cable needles are short double pointed needles used to hold stitches temporarily when knitting cables.

Stitch holders resemble large safety pins and are also used to hold stitches, for example, around a neckline when the neckband stitches will be picked up and worked after the back and front have been joined. Alternatively, thread a contrast-coloured yarn through the stitches to be held while they are on the needle, then slip the stitches off the needle and knot both ends of the contrast yarn together.

Use **blunt pointed needles** for sewing completed pieces of knitting together.

A row counter is a cylinder with a numbered dial that is pushed on to the needle and the dial is turned at the completion of each row.

A tape measure is essential for checking tension swatches and for measuring the length and width of completed knitting.

A crochet hook is useful for picking up dropped stitches.

Knitting Yarn

Yarn is the term used for strands of spun fibre which are twisted into a continuous thread of the required thickness. It can be of animal origin (wool, angora, mohair, silk), vegetable origin (cotton, linen) or man-made (nylon, acrylic, rayon).

Each strand of yarn is known as a ply. A number of plys are twisted together to form the yarn. The texture and characteristics of the yarn may be varied by the combination of fibres and by the way in which it is spun.

Buying Yarn

Yarn manufacturers wrap each ball with a paper band on which is printed a lot of necessary information. The ball band states the weight of the yarn and its composition, gives instructions for washing and ironing and may state the ideal range of needle sizes to be used with the yarn. It also carries the shade number and dye lot number and it is important that you use yarn of the same dye lot for a single project. Different dye lots vary subtly in shading which may not be apparent when you are holding two balls, but which will show as a variation in shade on the finished piece of knitting.

Always keep the ball band as a reference. Pin it to the tension swatch and keep them together with any left over yarn and spare buttons or other trimmings. That way you can always check the washing instructions and also have materials for repairs.

Basic Techniques

Holding the Needles

The right needle is held as if holding a pencil. For casting on and working the first few rows the knitted piece passes over the hand, between the thumb and the index finger. As work progresses let the thumb slide under the knitted piece, grasping the needle from below.

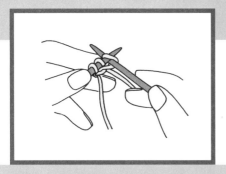

The left needle is held lightly, using the thumb and index finger to control the tip of the needle.

Holding the Yarn

There are various methods of winding the yarn round the fingers to control the tension on the yarn and so produce even knitting. In time you might develop a favourite way but first try the popular method shown here.

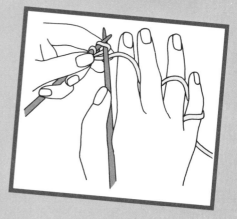

Holding yarn in right hand, pass under the little finger, then around same finger, over third finger, under centre finger and over index finger. The index finger is used to pass the yarn around the needle tip. The yarn circled around the little finger creates the necessary tension for knitting evenly.

Making a Slip Knot

A slip knot is the starting point for almost everything you do in knitting and is the basis of all casting on techniques.

1 Wind the yarn around two fingers and over the two fingers again to the back of the first thread.

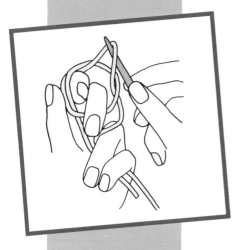

2 Using a knitting needle pull the back thread through the front one to form a loop.

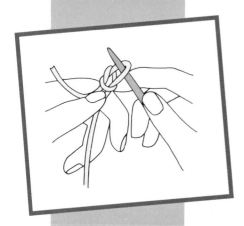

3 Pull end to tighten the loop.

Casting On

There are two common methods of casting on. The thumb method is used whenever a very elastic edge is required or when the rows immediately after the cast-on edge are to be worked in garter or stocking stitch. The second method is the cable or 'between stitches' method. This gives a firm neat finish and is best for use before ribbing or any other firm type of stitch.

Thumb Method

1 Make a slip knot about 1m (depending on the number of stitches required) from the end of the yarn. Hold the needle in the right hand with the ball end of the yarn over your first finger. *Wind the loose end of the yarn around the left thumb from front to back.

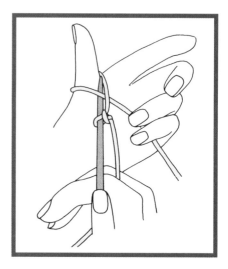

2 Insert the needle through the yarn on the thumb.

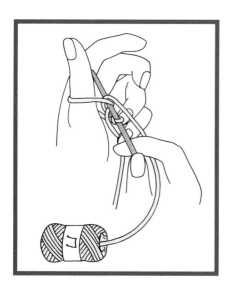

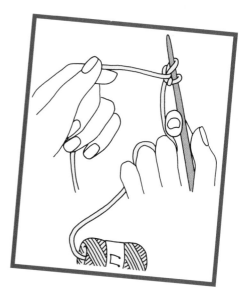

3 Take the ball end of yarn with your right forefinger over the needle point .

5 Remove your left thumb from the yarn and pull the loose end to secure the stitch.

Repeat from * until the required number of stitches has been cast on.

Cable Method

This method requires the use of two needles.

1 Make a slip knot about 10 cm from the end of the yarn.

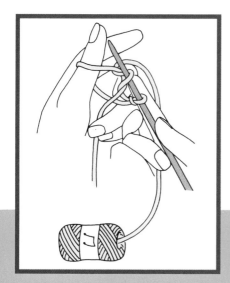

4 Pull a loop through to form the first stitch.

2 Insert right-hand needle through

the loop on left-hand needle and pass the yarn over the right needle.

3 Draw a loop through with the right-hand needle.

4 Place this loop on the left-hand needle.

5 Insert right-hand needle between

the two stitches on the left-hand needle. Wind yarn round point of right-hand needle.

6 Draw a loop through, place this loop on left-hand needle.

Repeat steps 5 and 6 until the required number of stitches has been cast on.

The Basic Stitches

Knit Stitches

1 Hold the needle with the cast on stitches in the left hand. With the yarn at back of work, insert the right-hand needle from left to right through the front of the first stitch on left-hand needle.

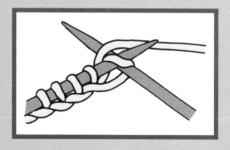

2 Wind the yarn from left to right over the point of the right-hand needle.

3 Draw the yarn back through the stitch, thus forming a loop on the right-hand needle.

4 Slip the original stitch off the left-hand needle.

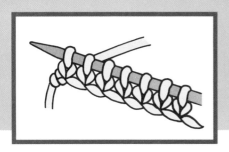

To knit a row, repeat steps 1 to 4 until all the stitches have been transferred from the left needle to the right needle. Turn the work and transfer the needle with the stitches on to the left hand to work the next row.

When every row is knitted (known as garter stitch) both sides of the fabric have raised horizontal ridges.

Purl Stitches

1 With the yarn at the front of the work insert the right-hand needle from right to left through the front of the first stitch on the left-hand needle.

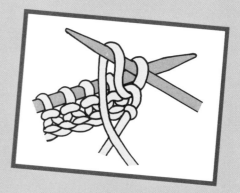

2 Wind the yarn from right to left over the point of the right-hand needle.

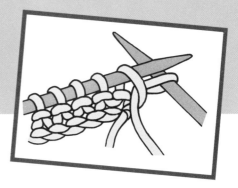

3 Draw a loop through on to the right-hand needle.

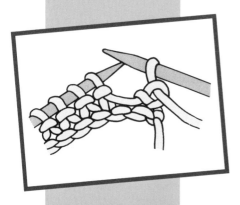

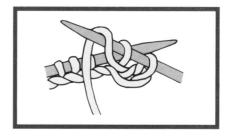

2 Bring the yarn forward to the front of the work between the needles and purl the next stitch.

4 Slip the original stitch off the left-hand needle.

To purl a row, repeat steps 1 to 4 until all the stitches are transferred to the right-hand needle, then turn the work and transfer the needles to work the next row.

Purling every row also gives garter stitch but can be slower to work.

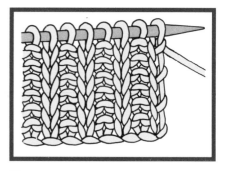

Stocking Stitch (st st)

Stocking stitch is the most widely knitted fabric, comprising of alternate knit and purl rows.

Single Rib (k1, p1)

This is formed by alternately knitting a stitch, then purling a stitch to give unbroken vertical lines on each side of the work. It is used for borders such as welts, neckbands and cuffs and is generally worked on a smaller size needle than the main body of the garment to keep it firm and elastic.

1 Knit the first stitch.

3 Take the yarn to the back of the work between the needles and knit the next stitch.

Repeat steps 2 and 3 until all stitches are transferred to the right-hand needle.

Always ensure that stitches which are knitted on one row are purled on the following row and vice versa.

Casting Off

Always cast off in pattern. This means that in stocking stitch you cast off knit-wise on a knit row and purlwise on a purl row. Casting off ribbing should always be done as if you were continuing to rib. Most pattern stitches can also be followed during the course of the casting off.

Casting Off Knitwise

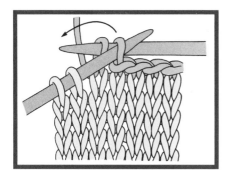

Knit the first two stitches. *Using the left-hand needle lift the first stitch over the second and drop it off the needle. Knit the next stitch and repeat from the * until all the stitches have been worked from the left-hand needle and one stitch only remains on the right-hand needle. Cut the yarn and thread the cut end through the stitch on the needle. Draw the yarn up firmly to fasten off the last stitch.

Shaping

A knitted fabric can be shaped to make it narrower or wider by decreasing or increasing the number of stitches on the needle.

Decreasing

The simplest method of decreasing one stitch is to work two stitches together.

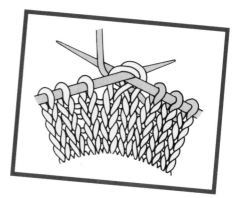

On a knit row insert the right-hand needle from left to right through two stitches instead of one, then knit them together as one stitch. This is called knit two together **(k2tog).**

On a purl row insert the right-hand needle from right to left through two stitches instead of one, then purl them together as one stitch. This is called purl two together **(p2tog).**

Increasing

The most usual method of increasing is to work twice into a stitch.

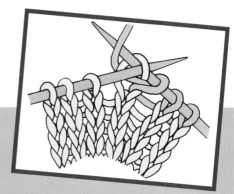

On a knit row work into the front and

back of a stitch as follows: knit into the stitch, then before slipping it off the needle, twist the right-hand needle behind the left-hand one and knit again into the back of the loop then slip the original stitch off the left-hand needle.

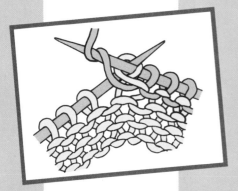

On a purl row the method is similar. Purl into the front of the stitch, then purl into the back of it before slipping it off the needle.

Making a Stitch

Another form of increasing involves working into the strand between two stitches and is usually called 'make one stitch' **(M1).**

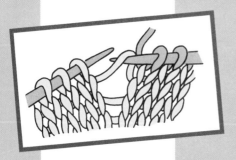

1 Insert the right-hand needle from

front to back under the horizontal strand which runs between the stitches on the needles.

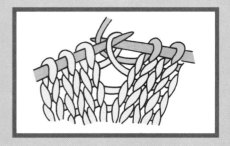

2 Insert the left-hand needle from front to back.

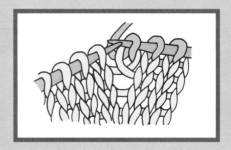

3 Knit or purl through the **back** of the strand twisting the new stitch to prevent the small hole forming.

Joining in New Yarn

Always join in a new ball of yarn at the start of a row wherever possible. If in doubt join in the new ball to avoid the frustration of running out of yarn in the middle of a row and having to unpick the stitches worked.

To make a perfect join at the edge of the work, simply drop the old yarn and start working the row with the new yarn. After a few stitches, tie the old and new ends in a loose knot. The ends can be darned into the seam at a later stage.

Slip Markers

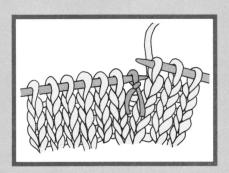

It is sometimes helpful to mark a panel or to separate a motif from the background fabric, or to mark the beginning/end of a round in circular knitting. Make a slip knot in a short length of contrasting yarn and place on needle where required. On the following rows slip the marker from one needle to the other on every row until the pattern is established and the marker is no longer required. For circular knitting, leave the marker in place throughout.

Correcting Dropped Stitches

A stitch dropped a few rows below the work on the needles can be picked up and re-created on each row as long as the work has not progressed too far.

However, if you have continued knitting, the stitches above the dropped stitch will be drawn too tightly across the back of the work to leave enough spare yarn to re-create the lost stitch. In this case it is recommended that you unravel the work to the point where the stitch was dropped and re-knit the unravelled rows.

The easiest method of picking up dropped stitches is to use a crochet hook. Always work with the knit side of the stitch facing you, so you might sometimes have to turn the work over depending on the pattern. Insert the hook into the free stitch from the front. With the hook pointing upwards, catch the first strand of the ladder from above and draw it through the stitch.

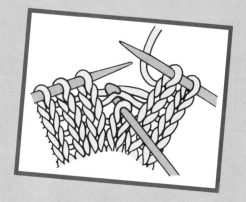

Continue in this way up the ladder until all the strands have been worked, then replace the stitch on the left-hand needle taking care not to twist it. If more than one stitch has dropped, secure the others with a safety pin until you are ready to pick them up.

Working from a Pattern

Before starting to knit your pattern read it through, this will give you an idea of how the pattern is structured. Patterns are written in a language all of their own. Abbreviations are used for many of the repetitive words which occur in the instructions, although not all publications use exactly the same abbreviations, the terminology will soon become familiar.

Abbreviations and Terms

The following terms and abbreviations are used in this publication.

Figures in round brackets ( ) refer to the larger sizes.

Figures or instructions in square brackets [ ] should be repeated as stated after the brackets.

The quantities of yarn are are based on average requirements and are therefore approximate.

For North American Readers

English terms are used throughout this book. Please note the equivalent American terms:
Cast off - Bind off
Stocking Stitch - Stockinette Stitch
Tension - Gauge
Yarn Over (yo) - Yf, Yfrn, Yon and Yrn (to make a stitch)

Alt = alternate; **beg** = beginning; **cm** = centimetres; **dec** = decrease; **dms** = double moss stitch; **inc** = increase; **ins** = inches; **k** = knit; **p** = purl; **psso** = pass slipped stitch over; **rep** = repeat; **sl** = slip; **st(s)** = stitch(es); **st st** = stocking stitch; **tog** = together; **tbl** = through back of loop; **yb** = yarn back; **yf** = yarn forward; **yfrn** = yarn forward round needle; **yrn** = yarn round needle.

Stitch Charts

Most knitters have already used charts to knit Fairisle or Intarsia patterns. We have given the stitches in this book both written and charted instructions in the hope that you will discover how useful charts can be for stitch patterns. A stitch chart also gives a visual impression of how the finished pattern will appear, enabling instructions for long and complicated patterns to be given in a clear and concise way.

How to Read Charts

Charts are read exactly as the knitting is worked - from the bottom to the top. After the last row has been worked repeat the sequence from the first row.

Each symbol represents an instruction. Symbols have been designed as far as possible to resemble the appearance of the knitting. However it is not always possible to be exact, therefore it is vital that you **always** refer to the detailed description of each symbol.

Before starting to knit look up all the symbols on your chosen chart so that you are familiar with the techniques involved. These are either shown with the pattern as a special abbreviation or with the general abbreviations.

Each square represents a stitch and each horizontal line a row. Place a ruler above the line you are working and work the symbols one by one. If you are new to chart reading you may find it helpful to compare the charted instructions with the written ones.

For knitters who wish to follow the written instructions it is still a good idea to look at the chart before starting, to see what the repeat looks like and how the pattern has been balanced.

Right and Wrong Side Rows

'Right side rows' are rows where the right side of the fabric is facing you when you work and 'wrong side rows' are rows where the wrong side of the fabric is facing you when you work. Row numbers are shown at the side of the charts **at the beginning of the row**.

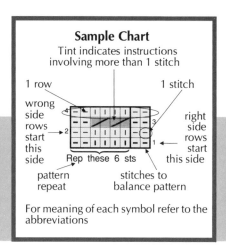

Sample Chart
Tint indicates instructions involving more than 1 stitch

1 row   1 stitch

wrong
side
rows
start
this
side

right
side
rows
start
this side

Rep these 6 sts

pattern   stitches to
repeat   balance pattern

For meaning of each symbol refer to the abbreviations

Right side rows are always read from right to left. Wrong side rows are always read from left to right.

Symbols on the charts are shown as they appear from the right side of the work. For example, a horizontal dash stands for a purl 'bump' on the right side regardless of whether it was achieved by purling on a right side row or knitting on a wrong side row.

Note: Symbols are dark on right side rows and light on wrong side rows. Make sure you understand the difference between working similar symbols on a right side row and a wrong side row.

Basic Symbols

ı	**K** knit on right side rows
−	**K** knit on wrong side rows
−	**P** purl on right side rows
ı	**P** purl on wrong side rows

Panels

A pattern panel is worked across a given number of stitches on a background of a contrasting stitch. To work any of the panels you must cast on enough stitches to work the panel plus the required number of background stitches each side.

All-over Patterns

An all-over pattern is one where the number of stitches given as a multiple is repeated and can be knitted across as narrow or wide a piece of the knitting as required.

43

Pattern Repeats and Multiples

The 'multiple' of each all-over pattern is given with each set of instructions, for example:- **'Multiple of 7 sts + 4'.** This means that you can cast on any number of stitches which is a multiple of 7 plus 4 stitches; for instance 14 + 4 sts, 21 + 4 sts, 28 + 4 sts etc.

In the written instructions the 7 stitches are shown in parentheses or brackets or follow an asterisk (shown as *), and these stitches are repeated across the row the required number of times. In charted instructions the multiple is indicated by a bracket at the bottom of the chart and heavier vertical lines. The extra stitches not included in the multiple are there to 'balance' the row or make it symmetrical and are only worked once.

Tension or Gauge

Knitting tension or gauge refers to the number of stitches and rows in a given area. You have to produce fabric with the same number of stitches and rows as given in the tension paragraph so that you obtain the correct measurements for the garment you intend to knit.

The needle size indicated in the pattern is the one which **most** knitters will use to achieve this tension, but it is the tension that is important, not the needle size.

The way to ensure that you do achieve a correct tension is to work a tension sample or swatch before starting the main part of the knitting.

Making a Tension Swatch

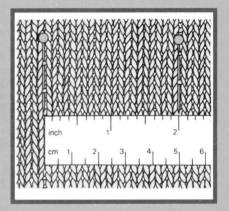

1 The instructions given in the tension paragraph of a pattern will be either over stocking stitch or the pattern stitch used for the garment. Cast on the correct multiple of stitches to be able to work the pattern for a swatch at least 12 cm [5 ins] in width. Work in the required pattern until the piece measures approximately 12 cm [5 ins], then break the yarn, thread it through the stitches and slip them off the needle. Do not cast off or measure the swatch while still on the needle as this could distort the stitches.

2 First measure the stitch tension across the centre of the swatch by counting the number of stitches stated in the pattern's recommended tension. Mark either end with pins. If your tension is correct the measurement between the pins should be the same as that stated in the pattern.

If the measurement is more, then your knitting is too loose, try making another swatch using smaller needles. If the measurement is less than required try making another swatch using larger needles.

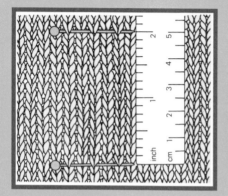

3 For the row tension count the number of rows recommended in the pattern vertically down the centre of the fabric avoiding the rows at the edges of the swatch. Mark with pins at each end and then check the distance between them. Once the stitch tension is right, the row tension is most likely to be correct. Any slight inaccuracies could be overlooked as the lengthwise proportions of a garment are **usually** given as a measurement.

Measuring a Garment

To measure a piece of knitting while it is in progress, spread the work out flat on a table. Never stretch the knitting and always ensure that the width measurement is correct before measuring the length. Unless otherwise stated, always measure widths horizontally and lengths vertically - never diagonally.

Finishing

The importance of the finishing stages of a garment should never be overlooked. Too often a garment can be spoilt by rushing the final stages, and the time and effort taken to knit it is wasted if the end result is unsatisfactory. A better appearance can be gained by pressing the separate pieces before sewing them together.

Always check the ball band for information on whether or not the yarn should be pressed - this should also tell you the heat setting of the iron and whether to use a dry or damp cloth.

Some types of knitting or parts of a garment are best left unpressed. Pressing may flatten the texture and blur the details, and can make the ribbing lose its elasticity.

If in any doubt about pressing, always try pressing the tension piece first to avoid spoiling the actual garment.

Pressing

The characteristics of yarns vary greatly and information for individual yarns is usually given on the ball band. If none is available use the following as a general guide.

Wool, cotton, linen and other natural yarns - press work on wrong side using hot iron and a damp cloth avoiding all ribbing.

Synthetics - press lightly on the wrong side using a **cool** iron and a dry cloth, avoiding all ribbing.

Picking up Stitches

Once the main body of the knitting is complete it is sometimes necessary to add an edging or border. These can be knitted separately and sewn on, but it is quicker and easier to pick up the stitches along the edges and knit directly into these.

It is important that the stitches are divided equally along the length of the fabric, and also that they are picked up **either** through a whole stitch **or** half a stitch throughout to ensure an even line along the edge.

To calculate how to pick up the stitches, lay the edge to be used straight and measure its length. Place a pin at the halfway point at right angles to the edge, then halve these distances again and again, so that the length is divided into eighths. Divide the given number of stitches by eight and pick up approximately this number in each section, check that the total number of stitches has been picked up at the end.

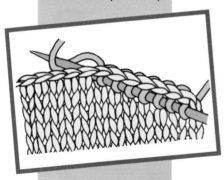

To pick stitches up along a cast-on/cast-off edge have the right side of the work facing you and insert the point of the right-hand needle from front to back under **both** loops of the cast on or cast off edge of first stitch, wind the yarn around the needle as though knitting a stitch and draw a loop through to form a new stitch on the needle. Continue in this way along the edge as required.

When picking up stitches along a side edge insert the point of the right-hand needle from front to back between the first and second stitch of the first row, a whole stitch in from edge. Alternatively, if the yarn is very thick work through the centre of the edge stitch, thus taking in only half a stitch.

Sewing Up

Use a blunt-ended needle and the yarn you have been knitting with for the seams unless it is thick or textured, then use a finer, toning coloured yarn.

Mattress Stitch Seam

1 With the right side facing you, lay the two pieces to be joined flat and edge to edge. Insert the needle between the edge stitch and the second stitch on the first row. Pass the needle under two rows, then bring it back through to the front.

2 Return to the opposite side and, working under **two** rows at a time throughout, repeat this zigzag action always taking the needle under the strands that correspond exactly to the other side, and going into the hole that the last stitch on that side came out of, taking care not to miss any rows.